THE LAZY BELIEVER

BY CYNDY GREEN

When I first felt in my heart that I needed to write a book called The Lazy Believer, I had no idea what a lazy believer was. I looked up the definition of lazy, read a couple of Christian sermons about laziness and slothfulness online, and read several scriptures in Proverbs.

I quickly discovered two things; one, laziness in one area of a person's natural, physical life can be an indicator of spiritual laziness, and two, I was a lazy believer!

Now I understand why the Lord instructed me to write this book! I needed to overcome in this area, and to share what I learned with other lazy believers so they could overcome.

This book is dedicated to all the people who love God and do not want to miss out on anything He has for them due to any reason, most especially laziness!

TABLE OF CONTENTS

CHAPTER ONE

WHAT IS A LAZY BELIEVER?

Lazy-Disinclined to action or exertion; naturally or habitually slothful; sluggish; indolent; averse to labor; heavy in motion. 2. Slow; moving slowly or apparently with labor; as a lazy stream.

Believer- One who believes; 1. In theology, one who gives credit to the truth of the scriptures, as a revelation from God. In a more restricted sense, a professor of Christianity; one who receives the gospel, as unfolding the true way of salvation, and Christ, as his Savior.
(Definitions: Webster's 1828 Dictionary)

A1 lazy believer is someone disinclined to action or exertion, someone who is slothful, sluggish, and averse to labor and yet believes the truth of the Word of God and receives the gospel of Jesus Christ. It would seem that these two terms, 'lazy' and 'believer', would be mutually exclusive. How can a person believe something and not act in accordance with that belief?

First, let's establish a basic, foundational truth; you are a spirit, you have a soul and you live in a physical body. When I talk about a person being a 'believer', I am referring to someone who has been born again and is a new creation, a person who has received the gospel of Jesus. Your physical body cannot go back into the womb and be born over again. Only your spirit can be born again, your soul (mind, will, emotions) and your body still need work.

John 3:1-7, 15-17 There was a man of the Pharisees, named Nicodemus, a ruler of the Jews: 2 The same came to Jesus by night, and said unto him, Rabbi, we know that thou art a teacher come from God: for no man can do these miracles that thou doest, except God be with him. 3 Jesus answered and said unto him, Verily, verily, I say unto thee, **Except a man be born again**, he cannot see the kingdom of God. 4 Nicodemus saith unto him, How can a man be born when he is old? can he enter the second time into his mother's womb, and be born? 5 Jesus answered, Verily, verily, I say unto thee, Except a man be born of water and of the Spirit, he cannot enter into the kingdom of God. 6 That which is born of the flesh is flesh; and that which is **born of the Spirit is spirit**. 7 Marvel not that I said unto thee, Ye must be born again.

15 That whosoever believeth in him should not perish, but have eternal life. 16 For God so loved the world, that he gave his only begotten Son, that whosoever believeth in him should not perish, but have everlasting life. 17 For God sent not his Son into the world to condemn the world; but that the world through him might be saved.

Believing is a heart thing, and actions, though they may start in the heart (spirit), they are filtered through the head (the soul, the mind, will and emotions) and then carried out by the physical body. You can believe something in your heart (spirit), but have doubt in your head (soul) and that will result in your actions not always lining up with what you truly believe in your heart.

Romans 10:9-10 That if thou shalt confess with thy mouth the Lord Jesus, and shalt **believe in thine heart** that God hath raised him from the dead, thou shalt be saved. 10 For with the heart man believeth unto righteousness; and with the mouth confession is made unto salvation

The disconnect between believing and doing is the result of laziness, spiritual laziness. It is the difference between being a doer of the Word and being a hearer of the Word only. James says that the one who hears the word but does not do the word *deceives himself.* So can laziness be connected to deception? I believe it can and it is.

Let's look at some scriptures that talk about laziness (slothfulness).

Proverbs 18:9
He also that is *slothful in his work is brother to him that is a great waster.
(* Concordance & Definitions pgs. 32-34)

Laziness and slothfulness are connected with being wasteful, hungry, without understanding, **dull of hearing** and not achieving your full potential. Slothfulness causes some to need to be taught the basic principles of the word over again instead of teaching the word themselves like they should.

The way of the slothful is as a hedge

of thorns. Have you ever tried to walk through a hedge made of thorn bushes? It is extremely difficult and very painful! The slothful person is making his way more difficult than it has to be. Proverbs 15:19 says the way of the righteous is made plain. Plain in the Strong's Concordance is a verb meaning to lift up, exalt, to cast up a highway. The righteous, the one who is in right standing with God (that is us if we are born again) has their way made plain, lifted up like a highway.

Proverbs 15:19
The way of the slothful man is as an hedge of thorns: but the way of the righteous is made plain.

Proverbs 10:4 He becometh poor that dealeth with a **slack hand**: but the hand of the diligent maketh rich.

Proverbs 24:30-31 I went by the field of the slothful, and by the vineyard of the **man void of understanding**;
And, lo, it was all grown over with thorns, and nettles had covered the face thereof, and the stone wall thereof was broken down.

I believe the field and the vineyard represent the harvest and the production, the prosperity, of the person in Proverbs 24:30. This slothful person's field was grown over and full of thorns; in other words, it was unproductive.

The field can also represent that person's sphere of influence, the part of the world that touches him, and that he effects. Thorns hinder growth, they choke the word. Look at Matthew 13:22.

Matthew 13:22 He also that received seed among the thorns is he that heareth the word; and the care of this world, and the deceitfulness of riches, choke the word, and he becometh unfruitful.

The laziness of the person in Proverbs 24:30-31 caused him to be unfruitful. Perhaps he let the cares of the world and deceitfulness of riches deceive him into making excuses and those excuses clouded his understanding and resulted in a reduced or nonexistent harvest?

This verse in Proverbs 24 goes on to describe the slothful man as a man void of understanding. Lacking in sense would be another way to phrase this. If the slothful man had some understanding, he would not have been slothful and let his field and vineyard slip into such a state. He would have known better.

Ecclesiastes 10:18
By much slothfulness the building *decayeth; and through idleness of the hands the house droppeth through

Hebrews 5:11-12
Amplified Bible (AMP)
Concerning this we have much to say which is hard to explain, since you have become ***dull** in your [spiritual] hearing and **sluggish [even slothful in achieving spiritual insight].**
12 For even though by this time you *ought to be teaching others, you actually need someone to teach you over again the very first principles of God's Word. You have come to need milk, not solid food.

Hebrews 5:11-13
King James Version (KJV) Of whom we have many things to say, and hard to be uttered, seeing ye are **dull** of hearing. 12 For when for the time ye **ought** to be teachers, ye have need that one teach you again which be the first principles of the

oracles of God; and are become such as have need of milk, and not of strong meat. 13 For every one that useth milk is unskillful in the word of righteousness: for he is a babe.

Proverbs 19:15
Slothfulness casteth into a deep sleep; and an *idle soul shall suffer hunger.

Psalm 120:2 Deliver my soul, O LORD, from lying lips, and from a *deceitful tongue.

The Hebrew word translated "deceitful" in this verse was translated as "idle" in Proverbs19:15.

Deceitful tongue equal to idle soul? Notice that slothfulness puts a person into a deep sleep and the idle *soul* suffers hunger? The hunger is caused by the soul being idle. The soul is the mind, will, and emotions part of you. This is where you think, imagine, plan, design, decide and experience 'feelings'.

Idle (definition from online dictionary)- without purpose or effect; pointless; (to) spend time doing nothing

Hunger (definition from online dictionary and Merriam-Webster)-have a strong desire or craving for;
A: a craving or urgent need for food or a specific nutrient
B: an uneasy sensation occasioned by the lack of food
C: a weakened condition brought about by prolonged lack of food

We can say that an idle tongue is the same as a deceitful tongue. An idle tongue is one that speaks without purpose or effect or says things that are pointless. An idle tongue is also one that spends time doing nothing. The mouth of the righteous speaks wisdom and is a well of life; the mouth of the idle (lazy, deceitful) either speaks pointless words without a good purpose or nothing at all.

Mark 11:23 For verily I say unto you, That whosoever shall say unto this mountain, Be thou removed, and be thou cast into the sea; and shall not doubt in his heart, but shall believe that those things which he saith shall come to pass; **he shall have whatsoever he saith**

What we say is what we get. Do

not allow a lazy, idle mouth to bring problems into your life. If you say nothing, that is what you will get. Nothing good, nothing productive, nothing blessed! Say what God says and you can have the promises. Speak fear, doubt, death, lack and you can have fear, doubt, death and lack!

Psalm 37:30 The mouth of the righteous speaketh wisdom, and his tongue talketh of judgment.

Proverbs 10:11 The mouth of a righteous man is a well of life: but violence covereth the mouth of the wicked.

Look at Proverbs 19:15 again. If a person is asleep, they are not aware of what is going on around them. A sleeping person is easily overcome by an enemy.

Pay attention to the number of verses that mention slothfulness and sleep or slumber. The slothful, sleeping sluggard will have poverty and be in want. The sleeping Christian, the one who is spiritually unaware and not alert, will not only miss out on what Jesus wants to do in their lives, but will not be effective in helping others.

Psalm 101:7 He that worketh deceit shall not dwell within my house;

Deceit (Concordance) - remissness, treachery, **laxness, slackness.**
The same was word also translated slothful in the following two verses.

Proverbs 12:24, 27. The hand of the diligent shall bear rule: but the slothful shall be under tribute. 27 The slothful man roasteth not that which he took in hunting: but the substance of a diligent man is precious.

Proverbs 26:13-16 The slothful man saith, There is a lion in the way; a lion is in the streets. 14 As the door turneth upon his hinges, so doth the slothful upon his bed. 15 The slothful hideth his hand in his bosom; it grieveth him to bring it again to his mouth. 16 The sluggard is wiser in his own conceit than seven men that can render a reason.

Proverbs 6:6-11 Go to the ant, thou sluggard; consider her ways and be wise: 7 which having no guide, overseer, or ruler, 8 Provideth her meat in the summer, and gathereth her food in the harvest. 9 How long wilt thou sleep, O sluggard? When wilt thou arise out of thy sleep? 10 Yet a little sleep, a little slumber, a little folding of the hands to sleep: 11 so shall thy poverty come as one that travelleth, and thy want as an armed man.

Proverbs 20:4 The sluggard will not plow by reason of the cold; therefore shall he beg in harvest, and have nothing.

The sluggard makes excuses. "There's a lion in the streets; it's too cold outside." Lazy people will always have an excuse for why they are not doing something that they should do. A lazy believer will also always have excuses. The sluggard says it's too cold and therefore does not prepare the ground at the appropriate time. He will have no harvest.

Excuses will always keep us from experiencing God's best in our lives.

TOP EXCUSES OF A LAZY BELIEVER
1. I can't.
2. I don't know how.

3. I'm afraid.
4. I'm not sure this is from God.
5. I don't have time.
6. I intend to do that someday.
7. I tried that and it did not work.
8. No one else is doing this.
9. Everyone else is doing this.
10.   I don't feel like it.

Most of us have used excuses at one time or another. The problem arises when we allow ourselves to make excuses for not doing what God wants us to do. To disobey God is sin. My excuse for disobeying God, for not being a doer of the Word of God, does not change that fact. Sin will separate you from God.

James says that the one who hears the word but does not do the word deceives himself. If you think you can skip being a doer of the Word of God, you are deceiving yourself. You are lying to yourself. Lying to yourself is just excusing yourself for bad behavior. No one likes being lied to. What if you lie to yourself? Is that any better? No, it is not.

James 1:22 But be ye doers of the word, and not hearers only, deceiving your own selves.

Proverbs 19:15 (AMP) Slothfulness casts one into a deep sleep, and the idle person shall suffer hunger.

Matthew 25:14-30 (AMP) 14 For it is like a man who was about to take a long journey, and he called his servants together and entrusted them with his property.
15 To one he gave five talents [probably about $5,000], to another two, to another one—to each in proportion to his own personal ability. Then he departed and left the country.
16 He who had received the five talents went at once and traded with them, and he gained five talents more.
17 And likewise he who had received the two talents—he also gained two talents more.
18 But he who had received the one talent went and dug a hole in the ground and hid his master's money.
19 Now after a long time the master of those servants returned and settled accounts with them.
20 And he who had received the five talents came and brought him five more, saying, Master, you entrusted to me five

talents; see, here I have gained five talents more.

21 His master said to him, Well done, you upright (honorable, admirable) and faithful servant! You have been faithful and trustworthy over a little; I will put you in charge of much. Enter into and share the joy (the delight, the blessedness) which your master enjoys.

22 And he also who had the two talents came forward, saying, Master, you entrusted two talents to me; here I have gained two talents more.

23 His master said to him, Well done, you upright (honorable, admirable) and faithful servant! You have been faithful and trustworthy over a little; I will put you in charge of much. Enter into and share the joy (the delight, the blessedness) which your master enjoys.

24 He who had received one talent also came forward, saying, Master, I knew you to be a harsh and hard man, reaping where you did not sow, and gathering where you had not winnowed [the grain].

25 So I was **afraid**, and I went and **hid** your talent in the ground. Here you have what is your own.

26 But his master answered him, **You wicked and lazy and idle servant!** Did

you indeed know that I reap where I have not sowed and gather [grain] where I have not winnowed?

27 Then you should have **invested** my money with the bankers, and at my coming I would have received what was my own with interest.

28 So take the talent away from him and give it to the one who has the ten talents.

29 For to everyone who has will more be given, and he will be furnished richly so that he will have an abundance; but from the one who does not have, even what he does have will be taken away.

30 And throw the **good-for-nothing** servant into the outer darkness; there will be weeping and grinding of teeth.

This is a very interesting story. The servant who did **not multiply** what was given to him, was called wicked, *lazy, idle and good-for-nothing!* I noticed a couple of things while studying these verses.

1. The servant was **afraid.** Fear NEVER produces anything good. Fear will always hold you back from achieving the fullness of what God wants for your life. This master gave to his servants in proportion to each one's own personal ability; so all

three servants had the ability to produce, to multiply. The third servant allowed fear to paralyze him and stop his production.

2. This servant **hid** what his master had given him. If I hide something from you, you cannot see it, or experience it. When this servant hid the talent he *prevented anyone else benefiting from it.*

Hebrews 6:12 (AMP) In order that you may not grow disinterested and become [spiritual] sluggards, but imitators, behaving as do those who through faith (by their leaning of the entire personality on God in Christ in absolute trust and confidence in His power, wisdom, and goodness) and by practice of patient endurance and waiting are [now] inheriting the promises.

Hebrews 6:12 (KJV)
That ye be not slothful, but followers of them who through faith and patience inherit the promises.

Be followers or imitators. Slothfulness hinders our ability to follow and imitate those who inherit the promises. Spiritual sluggards do not practice faith and patient endurance like they should. It requires *effort* to *follow* someone. The people who are inheriting the promises of God are **DOERS** of the word. They are DOING SOMETHING. Sluggards do not like to DO, they prefer to observe or be a spectator. Sluggards want to receive, they just do not want to *do* what is *required* to receive.

CHAPTER TWO

HOW TO OVERCOME SLOTHFULNESS.

Proverbs 6:6-11 Go **to the ant**, thou sluggard; ***consider her ways**, and **be wise**: 7 which having no guide, overseer, or ruler, 8 ***Provideth** her meat in the summer, and **gathereth** her food in the harvest. 9 How long wilt thou sleep, O sluggard? When wilt thou arise out of thy sleep?
10 Yet a little sleep, a little slumber, a little folding of the hands to sleep:
11 **So shall thy poverty come as one that travelleth, and thy want as an armed man**.

So, what does the lazy believer need to do first? Consider the ant's ways and **be wise**. Proverbs says the fear of the Lord is the beginning of wisdom. The first step is to develop the fear of the Lord in your life and repent of laziness.

Proverbs 9:10 The fear of the Lord is the beginning of wisdom: and the knowledge of the holy is understanding.

Proverbs 1:7 (Amp)
The reverent and worshipful fear of the Lord is the beginning and the principal and choice part of knowledge [its starting point and its essence]; but fools despise skillful and godly Wisdom, instruction, and discipline.

Prayer of Repentance

"Father, I come to you in the Name of Jesus, to confess the sin of laziness. I know being lazy is not your will for me. I repent; I change my mind and I change my attitude. I will not be lazy anymore. I will not allow my mouth, my words, my thoughts, or my actions to be lazy and slothful. I will make no excuses. I thank you for your forgiveness, and I choose right now to forgive myself. I am, right now, an energetic, prompt, faith-filled, faith-speaking, faith-doing person of God! Thank you, Father, in Jesus Name!"

Look at the ant, and understand

that you also will have to work. You will need to sow and you will need to reap. Sowing and reaping are both actions and require effort. There is a proper time to sow and a proper time to reap a harvest.

Know this: You already ARE sowing *something* and reaping a harvest from that which you have sown. If you sow laziness, inactivity, idleness or deceitfulness you will reap EXACTLY what you have sown. Remember the scripture 'God is not mocked, whatever a man sows, so also shall he reap'?

Galatians 6:7 Be not deceived; God is not mocked: for whatsoever a man soweth, that shall he also reap.

You sow it, you reap it that is a spiritual law. So take heed what you are sowing ALL THE TIME, not just what you pray for during your prayer time, but what you say all day and the actions you take. We should be living our lives ON PURPOSE. Do not just roll along, being pushed by every gust of wind or toss of the waves. Not living your life on purpose with a purpose is one of the quickest ways to find yourself living in a disaster area!

WHAT YOU NEED TO SOW.

1. A good confession.

What you say about yourself is very important. Now that you know you have been lazy it is time to begin to change that by changing what you say. Give up the excuses. Write all your old excuses on a piece of paper and throw it away or burn it. Just get rid of them! Stop saying 'I can't, I'm afraid, I don't know how' and start saying what God's word says about you.

2. Effort.

Every seed reproduces after its own kind. If you want to reap a harvest of tomatoes you do not plant carrot seeds, you plant tomato seeds. As you sow effort, it will grow and produce more effort. You may only have a small amount of effort to begin with, but as you put forth that effort it will increase. What I am saying is this; you might only have enough in you to read a few verses a day or to pray for ten minutes, but as you expend the effort to do this, faithfully every day, it will increase.

You will need to wake up, be alert,

pay attention! Being spiritually asleep is dangerous! We have an enemy in this world, and if we are not awake, aware and alert that enemy will run over us.

Billye Brim, a well-known minister and prayer warrior, has taught about America needing an awakening to God. The church, which is us, the Body of Christ, needs to be awake. We must be awake, aware and alert so we can hear God's voice, and be about His business!

How can we be a blessing to our families, friends, co-workers, and neighbors if we are spiritually sluggish? This life that you are living is not just about YOU. You are not the center of the universe. You are here for a reason and you do have a purpose.

No one fulfills their purpose while sleeping! So, wake up!

Look at Proverbs 6:7 again, 7 which having no guide, overseer, or ruler. The ant does what he is supposed to do and does not have constant supervision. When we know what we are supposed to be doing, we need to do it.

I have known people who only work when they are being paid to work and then only when their supervisor is looking. That is lazy and deceitful. Now that you have repented of laziness, it is time to not only work, but work when no one else is looking. Do what is right because it is right and not just because someone else is watching you.

Psalm 94:12 Blessed (happy, fortunate, to be envied) is the man whom you *discipline and instruct, O Lord, and teach out of your law

Hebrews 12:5-13 And have you [completely] forgotten the divine word of appeal and encouragement in which you are reasoned with and addressed as sons? My son, do not think lightly or scorn to submit to the **correction and discipline** of the Lord, nor lose courage and give up and faint when you are reproved or corrected by Him;
6 For the Lord corrects and disciplines everyone whom He loves, and He punishes, even scourges, every son whom He accepts and welcomes to His heart and cherishes.
7 You must ***submit to and endure** [correction] for discipline; God is dealing with you as with sons. For what son is there whom his father does not [thus] train and correct and discipline?

8 Now if you are exempt from correction and left without discipline in which all [of God's children] share, then you are illegitimate offspring and not true sons [at all].

9 Moreover, we have had earthly fathers who disciplined us and we yielded [to them] and respected [them for training us]. Shall we not much more cheerfully submit to the Father of spirits and so [truly] live?

10 For [our earthly fathers] disciplined us for only a short period of time and chastised us as seemed proper and good to them; but He disciplines us for our certain good, that we may become sharers in His own holiness.

11 For the time being no discipline brings joy, but seems grievous and painful; but afterwards it yields a peaceable fruit of righteousness to those who have been **trained** by it [a harvest of fruit which consists in righteousness—in conformity to God's will in purpose, thought, and action, resulting in right living and right standing with God].

12 So then, brace up and reinvigorate and set right your **slackened and weakened and drooping hands and strengthen your feeble and palsied and tottering**

knees,
13 And cut through and make firm and
plain and smooth, straight paths for your
feet [yes, make them safe and upright and
happy paths that go in the right direction],
so that the lame and halting [limbs] may
not be put out of joint, but rather may be
cured.

Psalm 94:12 says the man that is
disciplined and instructed by the Lord is
BLESSED. The Lord disciplines those
whom He loves. He instructs us in the way
of righteousness (the way of living and
being right) because he loves us and has
only good plans for us.

You want to experience The Blessing
in your life? One step is to receive the
discipline and instruction of the Lord. If
you refuse to be disciplined by God, then
you are not a child of God.

Proverbs says if you love your son
you will discipline him diligently. God is a
good Father and is diligent to discipline us
according to His word. We receive
discipline from our Heavenly Father
through the Word of God.

We need to patiently accept the
authority of God in our lives. He is the
first and last, the beginning and the end,

and He is the FINAL AUTHORITY and has final say in our lives. If His Word says to do something, DO IT. If the Word of God says NOT to do something, then (now this is really profound) DO NOT DO IT.

In order to know what we are supposed to be doing or not doing, we must spend time reading, meditating and listening to the Word of God and spend time in fellowship with God. How can you know someone, and know what they want from you and for you, if you do not meet them and spend time with them?

Clara Hayes, one of my pastors and a wonderful lady and teacher of the Word, taught me about getting closer to God. She said we must 'Practice His Presence'. Understand that God is omniscient, but that does not mean that everyone automatically experiences His Presence. We have to choose to acknowledge and receive Him.

Wherever you are, whatever you do, remember that God is with you. He is in you and around you and we can, at all times, connect with Him. We can be led, directed, instructed and corrected right now. This moment! He is not withholding anything good from us.

God inhabits (lives in) the praises of

His people. You want to experience His presence? One way is to praise. Begin to praise God from your heart. Welcome Him into your life by lovingly praising and worshipping Him. Praise changes your attitude and the very atmosphere around you.

1Corinthians 6:19 What? Know ye not that your body is the temple of the Holy Ghost which is in you, which ye have of God, and ye are not your own?

Hebrews 3:5-6 And Moses verily was faithful in all his house, as a servant, for a testimony of those things which were to be spoken after;
6 But Christ as a son over his own house; **whose house are we**, if we hold fast the confidence and the rejoicing of the hope firm unto the end.

You, if you are born again, do not belong to yourself, you belong to God. You are not your own. You are the temple of the Holy Spirit, a member of the household of Christ.

Take care of that which God has given you. You belong to God, He lives in you so do not dishonor Him with lazy, idle words and actions (or inaction).

Humble yourself. Simply trust God, believe the Word of God and get into agreement with Him. God says only good things about you because He believes in you! He has confidence that you will succeed. He has, after all, provided the way of success for you in His word.

I have found that, as I have begun to apply the things that I shared with you in this book, shaking off spiritual laziness is changing every aspect of my life. Focusing on not being spiritually lazy has caused me to also be more apt to avoid physical laziness. I believe that spiritual and physical laziness is connected.

Everything physical begins in the spirit. The more spiritually lazy I became, the less physically active and effective I was. Not being a doer of the Word will always lead a person in the wrong direction because you will be deceiving yourself.

Being deceived and making excuses in one area of your life causes other areas to be out of line. We cannot separate spiritual from physical when it comes to obeying God and fulfilling the call He has on each of our lives. We must line our lives, our actions and words up with His will, plan and design for us. Spirit, soul and body we belong to a loving, generous, wonderful Father God and when we do our part, He is *always faithful* to do His!

STEPS TO OVERCOMING LAZINESS

1. Fear the Lord and be wise.
2. Repent of laziness.
3. Sow a good confession.
4. Sow some effort.
5. Wake up! Be alert, aware and awake.
6. Receive the discipline and instruction of the Lord.
7. Practice His Presence.

More scriptures.
Proverbs 10:26 As vinegar to the teeth, and as smoke to the eyes, so is the sluggard to them that send him.

Proverbs 12:24 (AMP) The hand of the diligent will rule, but the slothful will be put to forced labor

Proverbs 21:25 (AMP) The desire of the slothful kills him, for his hands refuse to labor.

Christian-Christ-like.

STRONG'S CONCORDANCE (online)

Slothful (Concordance)-a. Inactive;
sluggish; lazy; indolent; idle.

Idle (Concordance)-remissness, treachery;
deceitful

Decayeth- to tumble in ruins
Droppeth through- to drip

Dull-slow, sluggish, indolent, dull, languid

Ought-to owe

Great-Concordance- ba al; a master
Waster-to decay, i.e. cause to ruin

Consider-to see, look at, inspect, perceive

Ways-way, road, distance, journey,
manner
Provideth-to be firm, be stable, be
established
Gathereth-to gather
Harvest- time of harvest

Strong's- Fools (Prov.1:7)-from a word
meaning to be perverse;
of one who despises wisdom
of one who mocks when guilty
of one who is quarrelsome
of one who is licentious

ONLINE DICTIONARY

Remissness- dictionary- laxness: the
quality of being lax and neglectful

Deceitful-definition-guilty of or involving
deceit; deceiving or misleading others
(malice from the will with forethought or
premeditation, thus from set purpose)

Idle-definition-without purpose or effect;
pointless

Fervent- boiling over with zeal for what is
good!
Serving- to obey and submit to
Business-earnestness, diligence,
earnestness in accomplishing, promoting,
or striving after anything

Perceive-definition-become aware or
conscious of (something); come to realize
or understand;

Correction- definition-the action or process of correcting something
Discipline-definition-the practice of training people to obey rules or a code of behavior, using punishment to correct disobedience.

Submit-definition-accept or yield to a superior force or to the authority or will of another person
Endure-definition-suffer (something painful or difficult) patiently.

Despise (definition)-feel contempt or a deep repugnance for.

Fool- definition-a person who acts unwisely or imprudently

Discipline (definition)-the practice of training people to obey rules or a code of behavior, using punishment to correct disobedience

Wisdom (definition)-the quality of having experience, knowledge, and good judgment; the quality of being wise. 2 The soundness of an action or decision with regard to the application of experience, knowledge, and good judgment. 3 The body of knowledge and principles that develops within a specified society or period.

Thank you for reading The Lazy Believer and I pray that this book has been a blessing to you and a help for you. If you enjoyed this book, please go to Amazon.com and leave a review, it would be very helpful and most appreciated!

Also, check out my blog, The Light of His Love.

For more books by Cyndy Green go to Cyndygreenbooks.com

God Bless You!
Cyndy

Made in the USA
Charleston, SC
30 September 2014